BEAUTIFUL Wild Flowers

BEAUTIFUL *Wild Flowers*

Southern Africa's floral wealth with its astonishing diversity of species – already more than 18 500 species have been discovered here – has intrigued botanists and delighted nature lovers for more than three centuries. This wealth of flowering plants is found in a variety of vegetation types falling in seven distinct natural areas, or biomes – from the desert wastes of the Namib to the evergreen forest biome of the southern Cape, KwaZulu-Natal and Mpumalanga. In the south the Cape boasts two unique biomes – fynbos and succulent karoo – each of which contains a very large proportion of plants found nowhere else in the world. Further north the nama-karoo, encompassing the Great Karoo and reaching up into Namibia, gives way to the grasslands and savanna that are more typically African. (Right) In spring one of southern Africa's most extravagant floral displays briefly transforms the otherwise harsh landscape of Namaqualand.

Der unvergleichliche Pflanzenreichtum Südafrikas mit seiner verblüffenden Artenvielfalt – mehr als 18 500 Spezies hat man hier schon entdeckt – fasziniert seit mehr als 300 Jahren die Botaniker und begeistert Naturfreunde. Diese außergewöhnliche Ansammlung von Blütengewächsen trifft man in unterschiedlichen Vegetationstypen an, die in sieben verschiedene Naturgebiete oder Biome klassifiziert wurden. Diese reichen von den Einöden der Namibwüste bis zu den immergrünen Wäldern des östlichen Subkontinents. Im Süden hat das Kap zwei einzigartige Biome aufzuweisen – Fynbos und die Sukkulenten-Karru – im Norden des Landes zieht sich die Nama-Karru, die die Große Karru einschließt, bis nach Namibia hinein, wo sie schließlich in Graslandschaft und Savanne übergeht. Leztere entspricht der Vorstellung, die man von einer typisch afrikanischen Landschaft hat. (Rechts) Im Frühling verzaubert eine überwältigende Blütenpracht, die eine der üppigsten Blumenwunder im südlichen Afrika darstellt, die ansonsten äußerst karge Landschaft des Namaqualands, das in farbenfreudiger Lebendigkeit erstrahlt.

La richesse florale incomparable de l'Afrique du Sud à sa diversité étonnante d'espèces – on en a déjà découvert plus de 18 500 espèces ici – intrigue les botanistes et enchante les amateurs de la nature depuis plus de trois siècles. Cette richesse extraordinaire de plantes fleurissantes se trouve dans une variété de types de végétation qui se divisent en sept régions naturelles distinctes, ou biomes – des déserts arides du Namib au biome de forêt à feuilles persistentes du sous-continent de l'est. Au sud le Cap est fière de deux biomes uniques – le fynbos et le karrou succulent – et plus au nord le nama-karrou, qui comprend le Grand Karrou et qui s'étend jusqu'a la Namibie, devient les prairies et la savane qui sont plus typiques de l'Afrique. (À droite) Au printemps un des déploiements floraux les plus extravagants transforme brièvement le paysage normalement dur du Namaqualand.

Fynbos is a unique vegetation type found only in the Cape, generally on very poor soils in areas with moderate to high winter or year-round rainfall. Three plant families – the Proteaceae (proteas), the Ericaceae (ericas, or Cape heaths) and the Restionaceae (restios or Cape reeds) are characteristic of fynbos. Both Leucospermum pluridens (above)*, one of the pincushions, and* Aulax cancellata *(male,* left) *with its needle-like leaves, belong to the well-known protea family.*

Fynbos ist eine einmalige Vegetationsart, die nur am Kap vorkommt. Die Pflanze wächst gewöhnlich ganzjährig oder im Winter in Gebieten mit nährstoffarmem Boden und Niederschlag. Drei Pflanzenarten sind charakteristisch für Fynbos: Proteen, Eriken (Kapheide) und Restien (Kapreet). Sowohl Leucospermum pluridens (oben)*, eine der Nadelkissen-Proteen, als auch* Aulax cancellata *(männl.,* links) *gehören zu dieser Familie.*

Le fynbos est un type de végétation unique qui ne se trouve qu'au Cap, en général aux sols très maigres aux régions à précipitations moyennes. Trois familles de plantes, – les Protéacées (protées), Ericacées (ericas, ou bruyères du Cap) et Restianacées (restios ou roseaux du Cap) sont typiques du fynbos. Leocospermum pluridens (ci-dessus)*, une des 'pincushions', ainsi qu'*Aulax cancellata *(mâle,* à gauche) *aux feuilles qui ressemblent aux aiguilles, appartiennent à la famille des protées.*

The members of the protea family, among them South Africa's national flower, the king protea, Protea cynaroides (right), *and* Leucadendron floridum *(male,* bottom*), form much of the shrubby component of fynbos. Both* Leucadendron *and* Aulax *species bear male and female flowers on separate plants. The woody cones of the female plants contain seeds which are often stored for years, until a fire destroys the plant and releases the seeds to start a new generation.*

Proteen machen einen Großteil der strauchartigen Gewächse des Fynbos aus. Die Königsprotea, Protea cynaroides (rechts)*, die Nationalblume Südafrikas, und die* Leucadendron floridum *(männl. Pflanze,* unten*) zählen dazu. Beide,* Leucadendron *als auch* Aulax*, entfalten ihre männlichen und weiblichen Blüten auf verschiedenen Pflanzen. Die Samen werden oft in der weiblichen Pflanze gelagert, bis ein Feuer sie freisetzt.*

Les membres de la famille protées, y compris la fleur nationale de L'Afrique du Sud, la 'king protea', Protea cynaroides (à droite)*, et* Leucadendron floridum *(mâle,* en bas*) forment une grande partie du composant d'arbustes du fynbos. Les Leucadendrons ainsi que les espèces d'*Aulax *portent des fleurs mâles et femelles sur des plantes différentes. Les cônes boisés des plantes femelles contiennent des graines, jusqu'à ce que la destruction de la plante par un incendie libère les graines, pour lancer une nouvelle génération.*

Another characteristic family of fynbos is the Ericaceae, also known as the Cape heaths. There are more than 650 Erica *species in fynbos, almost all of which are found only here. Some are beautiful individually, others are spectacular for their massed display of colour. Among the more striking species are* Erica daphniflora (opposite), E. macowanii (above left), E. mammosa (above right) *and* E. bruniades (left).

Eine weitere Komponente der Fynbos-Familie ist die Ericaceae, auch Kapheide genannt. Fynbos enthält mehr als 650 Erikaarten, die überwiegend am Kap vorkommen. Einige sind von individueller Schöhnheit, andere glänzen durch ihre Farbenpracht. Erica daphniflora *(gegenüber),* E. macowanii *(oben links),* E. mammosa *(oben rechts) und* E. bruniades *(links) sind einige Beispiele für diese schönen Pflanzen.*

*Une autre famille caractéristique du fynbos est les Ericacées, appelées aussi les bruyères du Cap. Il y a plus de 650 espèces d'*Erica *au fynbos, dont presque toutes ne se trouvent qu'ici. Quelques espèces sont belles individuellement, d'autres sont plus spectaculaires à cause de leur déploiement massé de couleurs. Parmi les espèces les plus jolies et les plus voyantes il y a* Erica daphniflora *(ci-contre),* E. macowanii *(en haut à gauche),* E. mammosa *(en haut à droite) et* E. bruniades *(à gauche).*

The Cape reeds (Restionaceae), the third characteristic component of fynbos vegetation, form the main understorey of fynbos, taking the place of the grasses found in other vegetation types. Like most restios, Elegia filacea (left) *bears male and female flowers on different plants. The rare* Podalyria tayloriana (below) *is a member of the legume family (Fabaceae), one of the largest fynbos plant families. Like many of its fynbos relatives, this plant grows from seed after fire.*

Die dritte charakteristische Komponente der Fynbosvegetation, das Kap-Reet (Restionaceae), bildet den Unterbau des Fynbos, d.h. ist das, was Gras für andere Vegetationsarten ist. Wie die meisten Restien hat auch Elegia filacea (links) *männliche und weibliche Blüten auf separaten Pflanzen.* Podalyria tayloriana (unten), *eine sehr seltene Leguminose, gehört zu den Fabaceaen, einer der größten Gattungen der Fynbosfamilie. Auch sie sprießen nach einem Feuer besonders gut.*

Le troisième composant caractéristique de la végétaton fynbos, les roseaux du Cap (Restiacées) forme la couche inférieure principale du fynbos, remplaçant les herbes des autres types de végétation. Comme la plupart des restios, Elegia filacea (à gauche) *porte des fleurs mâles et femelles aux plantes différentes.* Podalyria tayloriana (ci-dessous), *une plante très rare, est membre de la famille des légumineuses (Fabacées), une des plus grandes des familles de plantes de fynbos.*

Unique to fynbos is the Bruniaceae, here represented by Nebelia sphaerocephala (right)*. Like the Proteaceae this is an ancient family which exhibits an equally bewildering variety of flower forms and colours. Many of its species are rare and localized and the majority grow only on Table Mountain sandstone soils. The large red flower-heads of the red crassula,* Crassula coccinea (below)*, show up brilliantly among rocks on the mountains of the south-western Cape.*

Einzigartige Fynbospflanzen sind die Bruniaceaen, hier vertreten durch die Nebelia sphaerocephala (rechts)*. Wie die Proteaceae ist diese Gattung uralt und zeigt eine ebenso verwirrende Vielfalt an Blütenarten und -farben. Viele der Arten sind rar; die meisten gedeihen nur im Tafelberg-Sandstein. Die großen Blütenköpfe der roten* Crassula coccinea (unten) *bilden für zwei bis drei Wochen im Sommer leuchtende Farbtupfer auf den Bergen des südwestlichen Kaps.*

Unique au fynbos sont les Brunicées, représentées ici par Nebelia sphaerocephala (à droite)*. C'est une famille ancienne, qui montre une variété également déroutante de formes de fleurs et de couleurs. Beaucoup de ces espèces sont rares et ne poussent que sur les sols qui s'appellent les sols en grès de la Montagne de la Table. Les grands capitules de la* Crassula coccinea (ci-dessous) *ressortent d'une manière éclatante parmi les roches des montagnes du Cap du sud-ouest.*

Best known of the more than 200 orchid species in this region is the magnificent red disa, Disa uniflora (opposite, above)*, also known as the Pride of Table Mountain. This protected species flowers along mountain streams of the Western Cape in high summer. Its brilliant red colour attracts the Table Mountain Beauty butterfly which is responsible for pollinating this and other plants (including the red crassula) – all of which produce bright red flowers in summer.* Adenandra marginata (opposite, bottom left) *belongs to the citrus family (Rutaceae); like most of its relatives, the leaves of this plant give off a characteristic pungent smell when crushed.* Nivenia stokoei (opposite, bottom right) *is one of the woody Iridaceae, a small group with woody stems, found only in the fynbos of the Western Cape. Most woody irids are rare and thought to be survivors from a previous age. Also confined to fynbos is* Brachysiphon microphyllus (below)*, a recently discovered and rare plant found high up on the Touwsberg and Klein-Swartberg mountains in the Western Cape Province.*

Die bekannteste der über 200 Orchideenarten, die man hier antrifft, ist die wundervolle rote Disa, Disa uniflora (gegenüber oben)*, auch als 'Stolz des Tafelbergs' bekannt. Für nur knapp drei Wochen im Sommer blüht sie an Bergbächen im Westkap. Das leuchtende Rot zieht eine bestimmte Schmetterlingsart an, die diese und einige andere Pflanzen wie etwa die rote Crassula bestäuben.* Adenandra marginata (gegenüber, unten links) *gehört zur Zitrusfamilie (Rutaceae). Wie bei vielen anderen Pflanzen dieser Gattung verströmen die zerdrückten Blätter einen charakteristischen und starken Duft.* Nivenia stokoei (gegenüber, unten rechts) *zählt zu der holzigen Iridaceae, eine kleine Pflanzengruppe mit holzigen Stämmen, die man nur im Fynbos des Westkap findet. Die meisten holzigen Irisarten sind selten; man nimmt an, daß sie Überbleibsel einer vergangenen Ära sind.* Brachysiphon microphyllus (unten) *ist eine unlängst entdeckte, seltene Pflanze, die auf den hohen Berggipfeln des Touwsberg- und Klein Swartberg-Gebirges zu finden ist.*

La plus connue des plus de 200 espèces d'orchidées de cette région est la disa rouge magnifique, Disa uniflora (ci-contre, en haut)*, appelée aussi 'Pride of Table Mountain'. Cette espèce protégée fleurit le long des ruisseaux des montagnes du Cap de l'ouest en plein été. Sa couleur rouge brillante attire le papillon, 'Table Mountain Beauty', qui pollinise les plantes (aussi la crassule rouge) aux fleurs rouges en été.* Adenandra marginata (ci-contre, en bas à gauche) *appartient à la famille d'agrumes; comme la plupart de ses parents, les feuilles de cette plante émettent une odeur âcre caractéristique quand elles sont écrasées.* Nivenia stokoei (ci-contre, en bas à droite) *est une des Iridacées boisées, petit groupe aux tiges boisées qui se trouve seulement au fynbos du Cap de l'Ouest. La plupart des iridacées boisées sont rares et on suppose que ce sont des survivants d'une époque précédente. Aussi limitée au fynbos est* Brachysiphon microphyllus (ci-dessous)*, une plante rare et récemment découverte qui se trouve aux hauteurs des montagnes du Touwsberg et du Petit-Swartberg.*

Fire plays a crucial role in the rejuvenation of old fynbos plant communities. After a fire many bulbous plants, among them Watsonia angusta *(above) and* Brunsvigia marginata *(left, bottom), respond by flowering extravagantly the following season. In succeeding seasons, rapidly growing perennials like the sewejaartjie – literally 'lasting seven years' –* Edmondia sesamoides *(left, middle), and the wilde malva,* Pelargonium cucullatum *(left, top), flower profusely before they are crowded out by the slower-growing but eventually taller shrubs. They then die out, leaving their seed in the soil for the next fire cycle.*

Feuer spielt eine lebenswichtige Rolle bei der Verjüngung alter Pflanzengruppen des Fynbos. Viele Knollengewächse reagieren nach einem Brand mit außergewöhnlichem Blütenreichtum wie etwa Watsonia angusta (oben) *und* Brunsvigia marginata (links unten). *In den folgenden Jahreszeiten blühen dann schnellwachsende, pennerierende Pflanzen wie die Immortellen,* Edmondia sesamoides (links Mitte), *und wilde Geranien,* Pelargonium cucullatum (links oben), *ehe diese wiederum von den langsamer wachsenden, aber letztendlich größeren Sträuchern verdrängt werden. Die Blumen hinterlassen jedoch ihre Samen im Boden, die ein Brand eines Tages freisetzt.*

L'incendie joue un rôle critique dans le rajeunissement des vieilles communautés de plantes de fynbos. Après un incendie beaucoup de plantes bulbeuses, parmi elles Watsonia angusta (ci-dessus) *et* Brunsvigia marginata (ci-contre, en bas), *réagissent en fleurissant d'une manière extravagante. Pendant les saisons suivantes, des plantes vivaces qui poussent rapidement comme le 'sewejaartjie',* Edmondia sesamoides (ci-contre, centre), *et la malva sauvage,* Pelargonium cucullatum (ci-contre, en haut), *fleurissent profusément avant d'être remplacées à leur tour par des arbustes qui seront plus grands mais qui poussent moins vite.*

The coastal plains of the Western Cape carry two distinct vegetation types – sandveld on the sandy soils, and strandveld, a type of thicket, on limestone outcrops. The elandsvy, Carpobrotus sauerae (left)*, a succulent-leafed plant, grows in the strandveld where it forms large mats which are covered with deep magenta flowers. The Bokbaai vygie,* Dorotheanthus bellidiformis (above)*, and the leeubekkie,* Nemesia versicolor (right)*, are just two of the plants which transform the sandveld into a kaleidoscope of colour in spring.*

Die Küste der westlichen Kapregion beherbergt zwei klar umrissene Vegetationstypen: das Sandveld auf sandigem Boden und das Strandveld, eine Art Dickicht auf dem Kalkstein der Felsnasen und -kanten. Die Elenfeige, Carpobrotus sauerae (links)*, ist eine Sukkulentenpflanze des Strandveldes. Das Löwenmaul,* Nemesia versicolor (rechts)*, und* Dorotheanthus bellidiformis (oben) *verwandeln das Sandveld im Frühjahr in ein farbenprächtiges Kaleidoskop.*

Les plaines littorales du Cap Occidental portent deux types distinctes de végétation – le veldt sablonneux sur les sols sablonneux, et le veldt littoral, type de bosquets sur les saillies calcaires. 'L'elandsvy', Carpobrotus sauerae (à gauche)*, plante aux feuilles succulentes, pousse au veldt littoral. Le 'leeubekkie',* Nemesia versicolor (à droite)*, et le* Dorotheanthus bellidiformis (en haut) *transforment le veldt de sable dans un kaléidoscope de couleur au printemps.*

The drab appearance of renosterveld, a vegetation type restricted to the Cape and dominated by the grey renosterbos, Elytropappus rhinocerotis, *belies its wealth of very beautiful bulbous plants such as* Gladiolus liliaceus (left) *and* Moraea tulbaghensis (below). *These are just two of a host of individually spectacular flowers which appear in spring after the winter rains, when rising temperatures trigger new growth.*

Der eintönig graue Anblick des Renosterveldes (Rhinozerosbusch), eine Vegetationsform, die sich auf das Kap beschränkt und von dem fahlgrauen Strauch, Elytropappus rhinocerotis, *berherrscht wird, verbirgt die Blütenfülle seiner Knollengewächse:* Gladiolus liliaceus (links) *und* Moraea tulbaghensis (unten), *sind beides Irisgewächse. Diese Pflanzen sind zwei Beispiele für die Blumenvielfalt, die nach dem Winterregen wächst und sich entfaltet.*

L'apparence terne du renosterveld, type de végétation limité au Cap et dominé par le renosterbos gris, Elytropappus rhinocerotis, *dément sa richesse de très belles plantes bulbeuses comme* Gladiolus liliaceus (à gauche) *et* Moraea tulbaghensis (ci-desous). *Ce ne sont que deux d'une foule de fleurs individuellement spectaculaires qui paraissent au printemps après les pluies d'hiver quand les températures montantes provoquent la nouvelle poussée.*

As renosterveld grows on relatively rich soils, more than 95% of its original natural area has been replaced by agricultural lands. Floral treasures like Geissorhiza monanthos *(above) and the exceptionally coloured* Ixia viridiflora *(right) are correspondingly rare. Unknown numbers of renosterbos plants have been ploughed into extinction and those remaining are extremely vulnerable as there are no reserves which adequately conserve this vegetation type.*

Renosterveld wächst auf recht fruchtbarem Boden und wurde deshalb von der Landwirtschaft auf 95% seiner ursprünglichen Fläche verdrängt. Geissorhiza monanthos *(oben) und die außergewöhnlich farbenfreudige* Ixia viridiflora *(rechts) sind daher entsprechend rare Pflanzen. Ganze Flächen Renosterbusch wurden umgepflügt, und die verbliebenen Pflanzen sind gefährdet, da sie nicht unter Naturschutz stehen.*

Le renosterveld pousse sur des sols fertiles et a donc été remplacé par des terres agricoles sur plus de 95% de sa région naturelle originale. Des trésors floraux comme Geissorhiza monanthos *(en haut) et* Ixia viridiflora *(à droite) sont également rares. On ne sait pas combien de plantes de renosterbos ont disparues à cause du labourage; celles qui restent sont vulnérables car il n'y a pas de réserves qui protègent ce type de végétation.*

The veld around Niewoudtville on the Bokkeveld escarpment west of Calvinia is renowned for its springtime floral spectacle. A field of Bulbinella latifolia *(above), the unusually coloured* Hesperantha vaginata *(left) and a dense flowering of the deep red* Romulea monadelpha *(opposite bottom) all form part of this display, as do the pale yellow* Romulea montana *and the bright yellow* Spiloxene serrata (both opposite bottom)*. Unlike these plants,* Crinum variabile (opposite top) *flowers only in autumn; it is the only* Crinum *species which grows in the sub-continent's arid areas where it thrives in the damp beds of seasonally flowing streams.*

Die Umgebung von Niewoudtville, das auf der Schichtstufe des Bokkeveld und westlich von Calvinia liegt, ist berühmt für seine Blumenpracht. Weite Blumenfelder der Bulbinella latifolia *(oben), die außergewöhnlichen Farben der* Hesperantha vaginata *(links), der herrliche Blumenteppich der tiefroten* Romulea monadelpha *(rechts unten), sowie die zartgelbe* Romulea montana *(rechts unten) als auch die leuchtend gelben* Spiloxene serrata (rechts unten) *formen alle zusammen dieses einzigartige Blumengemälde.* Crinum variabile (rechts oben) *blüht hingegen nur im Herbst und ist die einzige Spezies der* Crinum*, die in den Halbwüstengebieten des Subkontinents gedeiht, wo sie in den feuchten Flußbetten der Trockenflüsse wächst.*

Le veldt autour de Niewoudtville sur l'escarpement du Bokkeveld à l'ouest de Calvinia est renommé pour son spectacle floral printanier. Un champs de Bulbinella latifolia (en haut)*, de l'*Hesperantha vaginata (à gauche) *de couleurs insolites, une fleuraison épaisse de* Romulea monadelpha (ci-contre, en bas) *rouge foncé , de* Romulea montana (ci-contre, en bas) *jaune clair et aussi de* Spiloxene serrata (ci-contre, en bas) *jaune vif sont tous des éléments de ce déploiement. Différant de ces plantes,* Crinum variabile (ci-contre en haut) *ne fleurit qu'en automne. C'est la seule espèce de Crinum qui pousse bien dans les régions arides du sous-continent, où elle prospère dans les lits humides des ruisseaux qui coulent saisonnièrement.*

The spring flowering of Namaqualand after good winter rains is one of the world's natural wonders, the more so since this is an otherwise harsh and dry land. (Below) *The annual daisies* Ursinia calenduliflora *(orange-yellow) and* Senecio cardaminifolius *(yellow) flower* en masse *in a sandy area. The soft, white flowers of* Colpias mollis (right) *bloom on a shrub that grows only in the crevices of granite boulders which are a characteristic feature of parts of Namaqualand.* Gladiolus equitans (far right) *also grows in granite, here in the rocks of the Kamiesberg mountains south of Springbok.*

Die kurzlebige Pracht der Frühlingsblumen im Namaqualand nach einem guten Winterregen ist zweifellos ein Naturwunder, vor allem, da dies sonst ein karger und trockener Landstrich ist. Diese überwältigende Blumenschau lockt Besucher aus der ganzen Welt an. (Unten) *Die gelb-orangene* Ursinia calenduliflora *und die gelbe* Senecio cardaminifolius *blühen auf sandigem Gelände. Die weichen, weißen Blüten der* Colpias mollis (rechts) *blühen auf einem Strauch, der in den Steinspalten der Granitfelsen wächst.* Gladiolus equitans (ganz rechts) *sprießt aus den Granitfelsen der Kamieskroonberge.*

La fleuraison printanière du Namaqualand après de bonnes pluies d'hiver est vue comme une des merveilles naturelles du monde, d'autant plus parce que c'est normalement une terre dure et sèche. (Ci-dessous) *Les marguerites* Ursinia calenduliflora *(orangé-jaune) et* Senecio cardaminifolius *(jaune) fleurissent dans une région sablonneuse. Les fleurs blanches et douces de* Colpias mollis (à droite) *fleurissent sur un arbuste qui ne pousse qu'aux crevasses des gros blocs de granit, caractéristiques des parties du Namaqualand.* Gladiolus equitans (l'extrême droite) *pousse aussi dans le granit des montagnes de Kamiesberg.*

Many of the perennials and woody shrubs of Namaqualand have evolved succulent leaves and stems which retain moisture, enabling them to survive the region's hot, desiccating summers. Most familiar of these, the mesembs (members of the Mesembryanthemaceae, called 'ice plants' in the USA) provide a brilliant counterpoint to the massed springtime colours of the daisies (above). *Very many mesemb species, known generally as 'vygies' ('little figs') grow in the succulent karoo biome. Among them* (left, from the top) *are* Cheiridopsis rostrata, Leipoldtia constricta, Lampranthus aureus *and* Carpobrotus quadrifidus. *These plants contribute in a significant way to the uniqueness of this vegetation type. Interestingly, their seeds are held tightly in the dried flowerheads throughout one or more summers until good rains fall and provide conditions suitable for germination. By not germinating every year, they avoid the possibility of being eradicated during one extremely dry season.*

Viele der pennerierenden und holzigen Sträucher der Sukkulenten-Karru im Namaqualand haben fleischige Blätter und Stämme entwickelt, die Feuchtigkeit speichern und es den Pflanzen ermöglichen, den heißen, trockenen Sommer dieser Region zu überstehen. Dazu zählen auch die Mittagsblumen (Mesembryanthemaceae), die ein schillerndes Gegenstück zu den großflächigen Frühlingsfarben der Gänseblümchen bilden (oben)*. In der Sukkulenten-Karru kommen viele Arten dieser Familie vor, darunter* (links, von oben nach unten) Cheiridopsis rostrata, Leipoldtia constricta, Lampranthus aureus *und* Carpobrotus quadrifidus*. Die Mittagsblumen sind ein unverwechselbarer Bestandteil und typisches Bild dieses einzigartigen Bioms. Die Samen dieser Pflanzen liegen in den trockenen Blütenköpfen oft mehrere Jahre lang brach, bis Regenfälle und weitere günstige Bedingungen die Samen der Pflanzen zum Keimen bringen.*

Beaucoup des plantes vivaces et des arbustes boisés du Namaqualand ont évolué des feuilles et des tiges grasses qui retiennent l'humidité ce qui les permet de survivre les étés chauds et séchants. Les mieux connues de ces plantes, les mesembs (membres des Mésembryanthémacées, appelées les ficoïdes cristallines aux Etats-Unis) font un contraste brillant avec les couleurs printanières massées des marguerites annuelles (ci-dessus)*. Le biome de karrou succulent a de nombreuses espèces de cette famille, appelées généralement 'vygies' ("petites figues"), dont* (à gauche, du haut jusqu'au bas) Cheiridopsis rostrata, Leipoldtia constricta, Lampranthus aureus *et* Carpobrotus quadrifidus*. Les mesembs font une grande contribution au caractère unique de ce type de végétation. Ce qui est intéressant c'est que les graines de ces plantes restent fermement dans les capitules pendant un ou plusieurs étés jusqu'à ce que la pluie tombe et crée des conditions favorables à la germination.*

The quiver tree, Aloe dichotoma (below)*, so called because the Khoisan once used the hollowed-out stems to hold their poisoned arrows, is a familiar feature of the more arid parts of Namaqualand. The largest of a number of local aloes, it produces yellow flowers in winter, which are pollinated by a variety of sunbirds attracted to the nectar. The tiny stone plant,* Conophytum pellucidum (opposite, top left)*, and another mesemb,* Ruschia evoluta (opposite, top right)*, have evolved to survive extreme temperatures on exposed rocks. The bobbejaantjie* Babiana crispa (opposite, bottom left) *and one of the sorrels,* Oxalis flava (opposite, bottom right)*, are two of a large number of bulbous plants whose underground storage organs enable them to endure the harsh summers of Namaqualand.*

Die Köcheraloe, Aloe dichotoma (unten)*, verdankt ihren Namen den Khoisan, die in den ausgehöhlten Stämmen ihre Giftpfeile aufbewahrten. Der Baum wächst in den ariden Gebieten des Namaqualands. Diese Aloe ist die größte der einheimischen Pflanzen. Im Winter hat sie gelbe Blüten, die die Vögel, die sich den Nektar holen, bestäuben. Die winzige* Conophytum pellucidum (gegenüber, oben links) *und eine andere Mesemb,* Ruschia evoluta (gegenüber, oben rechts)*, haben ihren Organismus derart verfeinert, daß sie die extremen Temperaturen auf Felsoberflächen überstehen können.* Babiana crispa (gegenüber, unten links) *und eine der Sauerampferpflanzen,* Oxalis flava (gegenüber, unten rechts)*, sind zwei Beispiele für Knollengewächse, die gelernt haben, den extremen Sommer des Namaqualandes zu überleben .*

Le 'quiver tree', Aloe dichotoma *(ci-contre), appelé ainsi parce que les Khoisan utilisaient les tiges creusées pour contenir leurs flèches empoisonnées, est caractéristique des parties plus arides du Namaqualand. Le plus grand d'un nombre d'aloès locaux, ses fleurs jaunes, produites en hiver, attirent une variété de 'sunbirds' qui pollinisent les fleurs en collectionnant le nectar. La toute petite* Conophytum pellucidum (ci-dessous à gauche), *et un autre mesemb,* Ruschia evoluta (ci-dessous à droite), *ont évolué pour survivre les températures extrêmes des roches sans abri. Le 'bobbejaantjie',* Babiana crispa (en bas à gauche) *et un des sorrels,* Oxalis flava (en bas à droite), *sont deux du grand nombre de plantes bulbeuses dont les organes souterrains leur permettent de survivre les étés durs du Namaqualand.*

Grielum humifusum (top) *often flowers in dense sheets of colour, its pale yellow, satin-textured blooms complementing the massed displays of springtime daisies, such as the widespread white rain daisy,* Dimorphotheca pluvialis (above). *Sometimes individual bulbous plants – like these* Lapeirousia silenoides (above right) *– flower alongside each other, creating a massed show among the rocks. The brief floral splendour of Namaqualand is in essence a frenetic competition by the plants to attract the attention of insect pollinators. This is vital to the production of a new crop of seeds which, depending on good rains, will eventually produce the next generation of plants. Unlike the daisies which are visited by a variety of beetles, bees and flies, the long, tubular flowers of* Lapeirousia silenoides *are pollinated by a species of long-tongued fly only.*

Grielum humifusum (ganz oben links) *bildet oft einen dichten, farbigen Blütenteppich in der flächendeckenden Blumenschau der Gänseblümchen, die im Namaqualand wachsen. Ein Beispiel ist die* Dimorphotheca pluvialis (links oben). *Einige dieser Knollengewächse,* Lapeirousia silenoides (rechts oben) *verbreiten eine üppige Blütenpracht zwischen den Felsen. Die kurzlebige Blüte des Frühlings im Namaqualand erinnert an einen frenetischer Wettbewerb der Pflanzen, die die Aufmerksamkeit der Bestäubungsinsekten auf sich ziehen zu wollen. Ohne die Bestäubung würde die Erzeugung neuer Samen verhindert, die während und nach der Regenzeit eine neue Generation an Pflanzen hervorbringt. Die Gänseblümchen werden von einer Vielzahl von Käfern, Bienen und Fliegen besucht, die langen Blütenkelche der* Lapeirosia silenoides *werden jedoch nur von einer einzigen, langzungigen Fliegenart bestäubt.*

Grielum humifusum (ci-contre, en haut) *fleurit souvent en feuilles épaisses de couleur, complétant les déploiements massés des marguerites printanières, comme la marguerite blanche répandue,* Dimorphotheca pluvialis (ci-contre, en bas)*. Quelquefois les plantes bulbeuses comme ces* Lapeirousia silenoides (ci-dessus) *poussent côte à côte créant un déploiement massé parmi les roches. La splendeur florale brève printanière représente une concurrence frénétique des plantes pour attirer l'attention des insectes qui les pollinisent. Elle est essentielle pour la production d'une nouvelle récolte de graines, qui, dépendant des pluies, produiront par la suite la prochaine génération de plantes. Différant des marguerites qui sont visitées par une variété de coléoptères, d'abeilles et de mouches, les fleurs tubulaires de* Lapeirousia silenoides *ne sont pollinisées que par une espèce de mouche à longue langue.*

The far north-western part of the Cape, which includes the Richtersveld, is a desolate stretch of land subject to extreme temperatures and gales. Among the more striking plants which survive these conditions is Hoodia gordonii *(left), a carrion flower, so named because its flowers smell of rotting flesh to attract flies for pollination.* Fenestraria rhopalophylla *(bottom left), a 'window plant', has transparent leaf tips which allow light in for photosynthesis without losing any water, and the spiny shrub* Sarcocaulon crassicaule *(bottom right) has succulent stems that store water, a characteristic shared by many of the Geraniaceae that grow there.*

Die äußerste Nordwestecke der Kapregion, die das Richtersveld einschließt, ist ein arides und ödes Gebiet, das extremen Temperaturschwankungen und peitschenden Winden ausgesetzt ist. Einige der ungewöhnlichen Pflanzen, die unter diesen Bedingungen leben, sind Hoodia gordonii *(links), eine Aasblume, die ihren Namen dem verwesenden Fleischgeruch verdankt, den die Blüten ausströmen, und* Fenestraria rhopalophylla *(unten links) mit ihren durchsichtigen Blattspitzen, die Licht zur Photosynthese ohne Wasserverlust einlassen, sowie* Sarcocaulon crassicaule *(unten rechts), ein stacheliger Strauch, dessen fleischigen Stämme Feuchtigkeit speichern.*

Le coin au nord-est du Cap, qui comprend le Richtersveld, est un terrain aride et vide, soumis aux températures extrêmes et aux vents forts et cinglants. Parmi les plantes les plus frappantes qui survivent ces conditions il y a Hoodia gordonii *(à gauche), fleur charogne, appelée ainsi parce que ses fleurs sentent la chair en pourriture pour attirer les mouches;* Fenestraria rhopalophylla *(à gauche, en bas), une fleur qui a des feuilles aux extrémités transparentes pour permettre l'entrée de la lumière pour la photosynthèse sans perdre de l'eau, et* Sarcocaulon crassicaule *(ci-dessous), arbuste épineux aux tiges succulentes qui accumulent de l'eau.*

A rather bizarre-looking plant of Namibia's extremely arid southern parts is the endangered halfmens, Pachypodium namaquanum (right)*, whose tall succulent stems carry but a small crown of leaves. The Khoisan people who once roamed freely in this area believed that these plants were transformed people, hence the name 'half-person'. Large specimens of this plant are very old; the one seen here has probably lived for more than one hundred years.* (Below) Pachypodium lealii *– only the flowers are seen here – is a related Namibian species which has adopted the same mode of growth in response to arid environmental conditions.*

Eine aufsehenerregende Pflanze im besonders ariden Süden Namibias ist die Halbmensch-Pflanze, Pachypodium namaquanum (rechts)*, deren hohe und fleischige Stämme von einer kleinen Blätterkrone abgeschlossen werden. Die Khoisan, die einst in diesem Gebiet umherzogen, glaubten, daß es sich bei den Pflanzen um verwandelte Menschen handele, daher stammt auch die Bezeichnung 'Halbmensch'.* (Unten) *Das Photo zeigt die Blüten einer weiteren, verwandten namibischen Spezies, nämlich der* Pachypodium lealii*, deren Wuchs dem des 'Halbmenschen' ähnlich ist und sich den harten Bedingungen der namibischen Landschaft angepaßt hat.*

Le 'halfmens' en danger, Pachypodium namaquanum (à droite) *est une plante d'aspect assez bizarre des régions australes extrêmement arides du Namaqualand, dont les tiges succulentes ne portent qu'une petite couronne de feuilles. De grands spécimens de cette plante sont très vieux; celui-ci vit probablement depuis plus de cent ans. Les peuples Khoisan qui erraient dans cette région croyaient que ces plantes représentaient des gens transformés, donc le nom 'demi-personne'.* (Ci-desous) *La photo montre les fleurs d'une autre espèce voisine de la Namibie* Pachypodium lealii*, qui s'est adaptée à la même manière de pousser, réaction aux conditions arides de l'environnement.*

The vast expanses of the Great Karoo, where sparse rains fall mainly in summer, are dominated by grassy nama-karoo vegetation ('nama-karoo' is an abbreviation of 'Namibia' and 'Great Karoo'). Further south, on the other side of the majestic Swartberg mountain range, lies the Little Karoo. Here, sparse year-round rainfall supports succulent karoo vegetation characterized by shrubs and woody perennials. The wild pommegranate, Rhigozum obovatum *(opposite), a shrub found in both Karoos, bursts into spectacular flower after rain. The kankerbos,* Sutherlandia frutescens *(above), a folk remedy for cancer, is widespread but* Nymania capensis *(top right), one of the chinese lanterns, occurs only in the Little Karoo; it is known more for its colourful seed pods than its flowers. The mesemb* Drosanthemum bicolor *(above right) is typical of the succulent vegetation of the Little Karoo.*

Die weiten Landstriche der Kleinen und Großen Karru, wo der geringe und unregelmäßige Regen überwiegend im Sommer fällt, werden von den Grasbüscheln der Nama-Karru dominiert. Die Bezeichnung 'Nama-Karru' ist eine Verschmelzung der Worte 'Namibia' und 'Große Karru', die dieses Biom umfaßt. Südlich der majestätischen Gebirgskette der Swartberge liegt die Kleine Karru, wo ein spärlicher Niederschlag die Vegetation von charakteristischen Sträuchern und holzigen Pflanzen ermöglicht. Der wilde Granatapfel, Rhigozum obovatum *(gegenüber), der in der gesamten Karru vorkommt, erstrahlt nach dem Regen in herrlicher Blütenpracht. Der 'Kankerbos' (Krebsbusch),* Sutherlandia frutescens *(oben links), ist weitverbreitet,* Nymania capensis *(ganz oben rechts) hingegen kommt nur in der Kleinen Karru vor;* Drosanthemum bicolor *(rechts unten) ist eine Mittagsblume der Kleinen Karru.*

Les étendues vastes du Grand Karrou, où la pluie éparse et irrégulière tombe surtout en été, sont dominées par la végétation herbeuse nama-karrou. Le terme 'nama-karrou' est une abréviation de 'Namibie' et de 'Grand Karrou' où ce type de végétation est dominant. De l'autre côté de la chaîne des montagnes Swartberg, est le Petit Karrou, où la précipitation éparse pendant toute l'année soutient la végétation succulente du karrou caractérisée par des arbustes et des plantes vivaces boisées. La grenade sauvage, Rhigozum obovatum *(ci-contre), fleurit d'une manière spectaculaire après la pluie.* Sutherlandia frutescens *(ci-dessus à gauche), médicament populaire contre le cancer, est répandu, mais* Nymania capensis *(en haut) ne se trouve qu'au Petit Karrou: elle est connue pour ses gousses colorées de graines. Le mesemb* Drosanthemum bicolor *(ci-dessus) est typique de la végétation du Petit Karrou.*

In stark contrast to southern Africa's arid expanses, the region's forests are confined to a few well-watered places in the southern and eastern Cape, KwaZulu-Natal and Mpumalanga. The Cape chestnut, Calodendrum capense (right), *in flower one of the most beautiful forest trees, ranges from the southern Cape north into tropical Africa. Perhaps the most spectacular forest flower, the forest lily,* Clivia miniata (below), *grows in deep shade in the evergreen forests of the north.*

In starkem Gegensatz zu den weitläufigen, ariden Gebieten im südlichen Afrika begrenzen sich die grünen Waldregionen auf Gegenden mit reichlichem Niederschlag. Die Kap-Kastanie, Calodendrum capense (rechts), *ist zur Blütezeit einer der schönsten Waldbäume; man findet den Baum vom Kap bis hinauf ins tropische Afrika. Die wohl prächtigste Blume des Waldes ist die Waldlilie,* Clivia miniata (unten), *die im tiefen Waldschatten in KwaZulu-Natal und Mpumalanga wächst.*

Contraste absolu avec les étendues arides de l'Afrique australe, les régions luxuriantes des forêts sont limitées aux endroits bien arrosés au Cap du sud et de l'est, au KwaZoulou-Natal et Mpumalanga. Le Châtaignier du Cap, Calodendrum capense (à droite) *un des plus beaux arbres en fleurissant, se trouve jusqu'à l'Afrique tropicale. La fleur des forêts la plus spectaculaire peut être le lis,* Clivia miniata (ci-dessous), *qui pousse à l'ombre profonde aux forêts du nord.*

Many beautiful flowering plants such as Crocosmia aurea (above), *well known in cultivation all over the world as montbretia, and* Dietes iridioides (left), *a close relative of the moraeas, grow on the fringes of forests where they thrive in the partial shade and moist conditions. The white iris-like flowers of* Dietes iridioides *are never seen in profusion; they are produced singly and last for only one day.*

Viele entzückende Blütengewächse wie etwa die Crocosmia aurea (oben), *die weltweit angepflanzt wird und als Montbretia bekannt ist, sowie die* Dietes iridioides (links), *eine enge Verwandte der Moraeas, wachsen am Waldrand, wo sie im feuchten Halbschatten gedeihen. Die kleinen, weißen, irisähnlichen Blüten der* Dietes iridioides *sieht man nie in großen Mengen; die Blüten dieser Blume wachsen einzeln und überdauern nur einen einzigen Tag.*

Beaucoup de belles plantes fleurissantes comme Crocosmia aurea (en haut), *bien connue en culture partout dans le monde comme la montbrétia, et* Dietes iridioides (à gauche), *parent proche des morées, poussent aux bords des forêts, où elles se développent bien à l'ombre partielle aux conditions humides. On ne voit jamais les fleurs blanches, qui ressemblent à l'iris, de* Dietes iridioides *à profusion; elles fleurissent individuellement et ne durent qu'un seul jour.*

The Eastern Cape Province is the meeting place of several vegetation types. Here savanna, widespread in Africa, meets the Cape fynbos and a thicket type of vegetation – known as valley bushveld – which is characteristic of this region. This is the home of one of South Africa's best-known plants, the elegant crane flower, Strelitzia reginae (above)*, now cultivated in most warm climates and particularly in California where it is the floral emblem of Los Angeles.*

Im Ostkap treffen verschiedene Vegetationstypen aufeinander. Hier begegnet die Savanne dem Kap-Fynbos und einer Art Dickicht, das als 'Valley Bushveld' bekannt und charakteristisch für diese Region ist. Es ist die Heimat der eleganten Paradiesvogelblume, Strelitzia reginae (oben)*. Nur in Südafrika kommt sie natürlich vor; in anderen warmen Regionen wird sie kultiviert, so zum Beispiel in Kalifornien, wo die Blume das Emblem der Stadt Los Angeles ist.*

Le Cap Oriental est le lieu de réunion de plusieurs types de végétation. Ici la savane, répandue en Afrique, rencontre le fynbos du Cap et un type de végétation aux bosquets appelée la brousse de la vallée, qui est caractéristique de cette région. C'est l'habitat naturel d'une des plantes les plus célèbres de l'Afrique du Sud: Strelitzia reginae (ci-dessus)*, ou le Paradisier. Ne poussant naturellement qu'en Afrique du Sud, il est cultivé aux plupart des climats chauds, surtout en Californie.*

The eastern coastal strip of South Africa is home to various plants well known in horticulture. One of these, the vlei lily, Crinum campanulatum (below left)*, is an unusual aquatic plant and one of several spectacular* Crinum *species found in the grasslands of the Eastern Cape Province. Others include the Cape honeysuckle,* Tecomaria capensis (below right)*; plumbago,* Plumbago auriculata (bottom left)*, and the striking flame lily,* Gloriosa superba (bottom right)*.*

Der östliche Küstenstreifen Südafrikas ist auch die Heimat anderer bekannter Gartenpflanzen wie der Tecomaria capensis (unten rechts)*; der leuchtenden Flammenlilie,* Gloriosa superba (ganz unten rechts)*, der* Plumbago auriculata (ganz unten links) *und der Teichlilie,* Crinum campanulatum (unten links)*, die eine ungewöhnliche Wasserpflanze ist und zu den prächtigen Crinumarten gehört, die in der Graslandschaft des Ostkaps gedeihen.*

La bande littorale orientale de l'Afrique du Sud est le domicile de diverses plantes bien connues à l'horticulture – le chèvrefeuille du Cap, Tecomaria capensis (ci-dessous à droite)*: le lis de couleurs brillantes,* Gloriosa superba (en bas)*, le plumbago,* Plumbago auriculata (en bas à gauche)*, et* Crinum campanulatum (ci-dessous à gauche)*, plante insolite aquatique et une de plusieurs espèces spectaculaires de* Crinum *qui se trouve aux prairies du Cap Oriental.*

The Lowveld, a sub-tropical area which encompasses the low-lying parts of southern Zimbabwe, the Northern Province and Mpumalanga, and includes the Kruger National Park, is dominated by trees. Many of these are beautiful in flower, such as the weeping schotia, Schotia brachypetala (above), *so named because its red flowers produce copious amounts of nectar – to the delight of numerous birds which visit the flowers and pollinate them.*

Das Lowveld, die nordöstliche Tiefebene Südafrikas, ist ein subtropisches Gebiet, das sich über die tiefer gelegenen Teile des südlichen Simbabwe, der Northern Province und Mpumalanga erstreckt und den Kruger-Nationalpark einschließt. Die Region ist eine baumreiche Landschaft. Sie bietet einen wunderschönen Anblick, wenn sie in Blüte steht: Die Schotia brachypetala (oben) *verdankt ihren Namen ihren nektarreichen Blüten, ein Paradis für Vögel.*

Le Lowveld, une région subtropicale de l'Afrique du Sud, qui comprend les régions basses du sud du Zimbabwe, la Province du Nord et Mpumalanga, y compris le Parc National Kruger, est dominé par des arbres. Beaucoup d'entre eux sont beaux en fleurissant, comme le "weeping Schotia", Schotia brachypetala (ci-dessus), *ainsi nommé parce que ses fleurs produisent des quantités copieuses de nectar, au grand plaisir de beaucoup d'oiseaux.*

In spring the flame creeper, Combretum microphyllum (top)*, provides brilliant splashes of colour along the streams and rivers of the Lowveld. Equally colourful, but flowering in winter, is the red and white impala lily,* Adenium multiflorum (above right)*, an otherwise drab shrub found in the drier, sandy parts of the Lowveld. Pride-of-De-Kaap,* Bauhinia galpinii (above left) *is a shrub well known in cultivation for its massed, vivid orange-pink flowers.*

Im Frühling sorgt die rote Rankpflanze, Combretum microphyllum (ganz oben)*, für leuchtende Farbtupfer an den Bächen und Flüssen des Lowvelds. Eine farbenfreudige Winterblume ist die rot-weiße Impalalilie (Wüstenrose),* Adenium multiflorum (oben rechts)*, die sonst ein farbloser Strauch in den trocknen Gebieten des Lowveld ist. Die* Bauhinia galpinii (oben links) *ist ein runder Strauch, der wegen seiner leuchtend rosa-orangen Blüten oft in Gärten angepflanzt wird.*

Au printemps Combretum microphyllum (en haut)*, fait des éclaboussements brillants de couleur le long des ruisseaux et des rivières du Lowveld. Également pittoresque, mais fleurissant en hiver, est 'l'impala lily' rouge et blanc,* Adenium multiflorum (ci-dessus à droite)*, normalement un arbuste terne qui se trouve aux parties sèches du Lowveld.* Bauhinia galpinii (ci-dessus à gauche) *est un arbuste arrondi bien connu dans la culture à cause de ses fleurs d'une couleur orangé-rose.*

Zimbabwe's flora shows the influence of tropical Africa. Like other members of the grape family, the Cyphostemma *species* (top) *is a scrambling shrub or climber. One of the morning glories,* Ipomoea shirambensis (above left) *is a creeper which flowers in spring. The well-known Zimbabwe creeper,* Podranea brycei (above right), *grows naturally only in Zimbabwe. The sparse vegetation of the Kalahari is transformed after good rains (which fall rarely). A species of* Tribulus (opposite) *briefly carpets the desert's red sands in an unusual floral display. This ephemeral herb exists only in seed form during the desert's long dry periods.*

In der Flora Simbabwes erkennt man das tropische Afrika. Wie andere Arten der Weinfamilie kommt die Spezies Cyphostemma (ganz oben) *als Kletterstrauch oder Rankpflanze vor. Eine der Winden,* Ipomoea shirambensis (oben links), *ist eine Kletterpflanze, die im Frühling blüht. Bekannt ist auch die* Podranea brycei (oben rechts), *die nur in Simbabwe natürlich wächst. Die spärliche Vegetation der Kalahari verändert sich nach einem guten Regen. Eine Art der* Tribulus (gegenüber) *bedeckt den roten Dünensand mit einem ungwöhnlichen Blumenteppich. Dieses kurzlebige Kraut überdauert als Samen lange Trockenperioden in der Wüste.*

La flore du Zimbabwe montre l'influence de l'Afrique tropicale. Comme les autres membres de la famille des Vitacées, l'espèce Cyphostemma (en haut), *est un grimpant rampant. Un des volubilis des jardins,* Ipomoea shirambensis (ci-dessus à gauche), *est un rampant qui fleurit au printemps. Un autre grimpant,* Podranea brycei (ci-dessus à droite), *pousse naturellement seulement au Zimbabwe. La végétation éparse du Kalahari est transformée après de bonnes pluies. Une espèce de* Tribulus (ci-contre) *couvre brièvement les sables rouges du désert d'un déploiement insolite floral. Cette herbe éphémère existe en forme de graine pendant les périodes sèches du désert.*

Grasslands cover the higher-lying parts of South Africa's eastern half, where winters are colder and summers milder than in the savanna region. This is home to the summer-flowering wild foxglove, Ceratotheca triloba (left)*, a low-growing shrub with aromatic leaves, which grows in open grasslands and along roadsides. Most parts of this plant are covered with fine hairs. One of the Christmas bells,* Littonia modesta (top left)*, a creeper with leaf tendrils, is found in shady spots. The wildekatjiepiering,* Rothmannia capensis (above)*, prefers rocky hillsides, kloofs or forest edges; in these relatively protected locations this small, evergreen tree safely avoids the frequent fires that break out on the open grasslands.*

Die höher gelegenen Gebiete der östlichen Regionen Südafrikas, wo der Winter kälter und die Sommer milder sind als in der Savanne, bestehen aus Grasland. Hier ist der wilde Fingerhut, Ceratotheca triloba (links)*, beheimatet, der im Sommer blüht und als niedriger Strauch mit aromatischen Blättern auf dem offenen Grasland vorkommt. Eines der Weihnachtsglöckchen,* Littonia modesta (oben links)*, ist eine Kletterpflanze mit Blattranken, die man in schattigen Ecken antrifft, während die* Rothmannia capensis (oben) *vorzugsweise auf felsigen Hügeln, in Schluchten oder am Waldrand wächst. In diesen relativ geschützten Standorten entgeht der kleine Baum den häufigen Feuerbränden der offenen Flächen.*

Des prairies couvrent les parties plus élevées de la moitié orientale de l'Afrique du Sud, où les hivers sont plus froids et les étés sont plus doux qu'à la savane. C'est le domicile de la digitale sauvage qui fleurit en été, Ceratotheca triloba (à gauche)*, arbuste bas aux feuilles aromatiques qui pousse aux prairies découvertes et aux bords des routes. Un des 'Christmas bells',* Littonia modesta (en haut, à gauche)*, grimpant aux feuilles à vrilles, se trouve aux endroits à l'ombre, tandis que le gardenia sauvage,* Rothmannia capensis (en haut)*, préfère les coteaux rocailleux, les 'kloofs' ou les bords des forêts. A ces endroits assez protégés, ce petit arbre à feuilles persistentes réussit à éviter les incendies fréquents des prairies découvertes.*

The yellow arum, Zantedeschia pentlandii *(above), grows in the open grasslands, generally amongst rocks. It is one of several species of* Zantedeschia, *popularly known as 'arum lilies', which have recently been hybridized to produce a range of garden plants with flower colours ranging from cream through yellow to red and pink. Like the wildekatjiepiering, the Mickey Mouse bush,* Ochna natalitia *(left), so called because its seeds resemble Mickey Mouse's ears, prefers rocky sites well out of reach of veld fires. Its small, black, roundish fruits are borne on fleshy red receptacles and are apparently quite irresistible to birds. These decorative fruits and the fragrant yellow flowers no doubt contribute to its popularity as a garden subject.*

Die gelbe Calla, Zantedeschia pentlandii *(oben), wächst im offenen Grasland und gewöhnlich zwischen den Felsen. Sie ist eine von mehreren* Zantedeschia, *die unlängst gekreuzt wurden, um eine Reihe neuer Gartengewächse zu entwickeln. Die Blumen variieren in ihren Farben von Crême über Gelb bis hin zum Rot und Rosa. Der 'Mickey-Maus-Busch',* Ochna natalitia *(links), der so heißt, weil seine Samen an die Ohren der Comicfigur von Walt Disney erinnern, ist ebenfalls ein Strauch, der felsige Standorte außerhalb des Feuerbereichs bevorzugt. Seine Frucht ist klein, schwarz und rund; sie sitzt auf einem fleischigen, roten Receptaculum, dem Vögel, so sagt man, kaum widerstehen können. Der Strauch ist eine beliebte Gartenpflanze.*

L'arum jaune, Zantedeschia pentlandii *(en haut), pousse aux prairies découvertes, généralement parmi les roches. C'est une de plusieurs espèces de* Zantedeschia *récemmment hybridisées pour créer une gamme de plantes de jardin des couleurs crème à jaune à rouge et rose. Comme le gardénia sauvage, le buisson de Mickey Mouse,* Ochna natalitia *(à gauche), ainsi appelé parce que ses graines ressemblent aux oreilles de Mickey, est un arbuste qui préfère aussi des lieux rocailleux bien loin des incendies du veldt. Son fruit petit, noir et assez rond, porté sur des récipients succulents, est apparemment irrésistible aux oiseaux. Ces fruits décoratifs et les fleurs jaunes fragrantes de la plante sont sans doute une des raisons pour son succès dans les jardins.*

When not in flower, hairbells like Dierama gracile (far left) *could well be mistaken for large tufts of grass.* Gladiolus crassifolius (left) *favours open grasslands, while* Protea laetans (bottom, far left), *a rare species discovered in 1970, is restricted to the mountains overlooking the Blyde River Poort on the Eastern Escarpment. The Barberton daisy,* Gerbera jamesonii (bottom left), *a protected species which grows naturally in the Barberton district and along the escarpment, has been developed to produce a variety of well-known garden hybrids. The vegetation on the quartzite rocks of Zimbabwe's Chimanimani mountains is reminiscent of Cape fynbos.* Leucospermum saxosum (below) *is a common shrub here.*

Wenn sie nicht in Blüte stehen, kann man die Haarglocken, so z.B. die Dierama gracile (ganz links), *sehr wohl mit Grasbüscheln verwechseln.* Gladiolus crassifolius (links) *bevorzugt offene Grasflächen; die* Protea laetans (unten, ganz links) *beschränkt sich hingegen auf die Berge, die die Blyde River Poort (Pforte) des östlichen Randgebirges dominieren. Die* Gerbera jamesonii (links unten) *ist eine geschützte Pflanzenart, die in der Umgebung von Barberton und entlang des Randgebirges vorkommt, und aus der eine Anzahl bekannter Kreuzungen hervorgingen. Die Vegetation auf dem Quarzgestein der Chimanimaniberge erinnert an Fynbos.* Leucospermum saxosum (unten) *ist ein in der Region weit verbreiteter Strauch.*

Quand elles ne fleurissent pas, les 'cloches velues' comme Dierama gracile (ci-contre, en haut à gauche) *peuvent être prises pour de grandes touffes d'herbe.* Gladiolus crassifolius (ci-contre, en haut à droite) *préfère les prairies découvertes, tandis que* Protea laetans (ci-contre, en bas à gauche) *est limitée aux montagnes qui donnent sur le Blyde River Poort.* Gerbera jamesonii (ci-contre, en bas à droite), *espèce protégée qui pousse naturellement dans la région de Barberton et le long de l'escarpement, a été développée pour créer une variété d'hybrides de jardins bien connus. La végétation des roches de quartzite des montagnes du Zimbabwe rappelle le fynbos du Cap.* Leucospermum saxosum (ci-dessous) *est un arbuste général ici.*

The escarpment forming the boundary between KwaZulu-Natal and the mountain kingdom of Lesotho is dominated by high basalt cliffs. This is the natural habitat of Ranunculus baurii (below)*, which is related to the well-known garden ranunculus. Lower down on the cave sandstone rocks, the Natal bottlebrush,* Greyia sutherlandii (right)*, a small gnarled tree, displays its masses of scarlet flower-spikes in late winter and early spring.*

Das Randgebirge, das die Grenze zwischen KwaZulu-Natal und dem Bergkönigreich Lesotho ausmacht, wird von hohen Basaltsteilhängen berherrscht. Hier ist die natürliche Heimat der Ranunculus baurii (unten)*, einer Verwandten der bekannten Garten-Ranunkel. Auf ausgehöhlten Sandsteinfelsen präsentiert sich die 'Flaschenbürste',* Greyia sutherlandii (rechts)*, ein kleiner, knorriger Baum, der im Spätwinter und zu Frühlingsanfang scharlachroten Blüten hat.*

L'escarpement qui forme la frontière entre le KwaZoulou-Natal et le royaume montagneux du Lesotho est dominé par des falaises élevées en basalte. C'est l'habitat naturel de Ranunculus baurii (ci-dessous) *parent de la renoncule de jardin bien connue. Plus bas sur les roches des cavernes de grès, le callistemon du Natal,* Greyia sutherlandii (à droite)*, un petit arbre noueux, déploie ses fleurs écarlates à la fin de l'hiver et au début du printemps.*

Kniphofia ritualis (right) *is one of several red hot pokers indigenous to the high grasslands and the escarpment of the Drakensberg. Also widespread in these grasslands, particularly in moist places and on rocky ridges, is the summer-flowering bulbous herb,* Eucomis autumnalis (bottom right), *one of the so-called pineapple flowers. Its erect inflorescence stalk with its densely packed flowers on short stalks, topped by a rosette of broad leaves, looks remarkably like a pineapple – hence the common name. Damp rocks high on the escarpment are home to one of the gems of the Drakensberg, the seldom-seen* Rhodohypoxis baurii (bottom left) *whose high tolerance to frost has made it a favourite with alpine gardeners overseas.*

Kniphofia ritualis (rechts) *ist eine von mehreren Fackellilien, die in den höher gelegenen Regionen des Graslands und entlang der Randgebirge der Drakensberge natürlich vorkommen. Ebenfalls im Grasland zu finden ist* Eucomis autumnalis (unten rechts), *ein Beispiel für die sogenannte 'Ananasblumen'. Diese Pflanze bevorzugt feuchte Gebiete und felsige Höhenrücken. Der hochaufgerichtete Blütenstand mit seinen dichtgepackten Blüten sitzt auf einem kurzen Stengel. Die Blume schließt in einer Rosette aus breiten Blättern ab, die sehr an eine Ananas erinnern – daher der Name. Feuchtes Felsgestein hoch oben auf dem Randgebirge ist die Heimat der seltenen* Rhodohypoxis baurii (unten links), *die viel Frost verträgt.*

La plante Kniphofia ritualis (à droite) *est un des tritomas indigènes aux prairies élevées et le long de l'escarpement du Drakensberg.* Eucomis autumnalis (ci-dessous à droite), *une herbe bulbeuse qui fleurit en été, et qui se trouve également dans ces prairies, surtout aux endroits humides aux arêtes rocailleuses, est un exemple des fleurs appelées les 'pineapple flowers'. Sa tige d'inflorescene droite aux fleurs serrées et nombreuses sur de petites tiges, couronnée d'une rosette de larges feuilles, ressemblent d'une manière frappante à l'ananas – donc son nom vulgaire. Des roches humides du haut de l'escarpement sont le domicile de* Rhodohypoxis baurii (ci-dessous à gauche), *rarement vu, et qui tolère bien le froid.*

The Natal red top grass, Melinis repens (below)*, one of the most striking of the Berg's grasses, provides swathes of red in the veld where it flowers in late summer.* Sandersonia aurantiaca (opposite)*, another of the Chinese lanterns, also called Christmas bells, is a creeper which climbs through the dense grasses alongside rivers and streams. In summer the banks of these streams are graced by the scarlet blooms of* Schizostylis coccinea (left)*. The Drakensberg is renowned for everlastings, like* Helichrysum adenocarpum (below left)*, whose hairy leaves and stems protect them from extreme cold.*

Das rote Gras Melinis repens (unten) *ist eine der hervorstechendsten Grasarten der Drakensberge. Wo es im Spätsommer blüht, meint man, rote Schwaden lägen über den Wiesen.* Sandersonia aurantiaca (gegenüber), *auch Weihnachtsglöckchen genannt, ist eine Kletterpflanze, die sich an den Flüssen und Bächen der Drakensberge im dichten Gras entlangrankt.* Schizostylis coccinea (links) *findet man auch entlang der Bachufer, wo die scharlachroten Blumen im Sommer blühen. Die Drakensberge sind berühmt für ihre Immortellen (Strohblumen),* Helichrysum adenocarpum (unten links)*.*

L'herbe rouge du Natal Melinis repens (en bas) *est parmi les plus frappantes des herbes du Berg, créant des bandes rouges au veldt où elle fleurit à la fin de l'été.* Sandersonia aurantiaca (ci-contre)*, une autre lanterne vénitienne, appelée aussi "Christmans bells", est un grimpant qui grimpe parmi les herbes épaisses le long des rivières et des ruisseaux du Drakensberg. En été les bords de ces rivières et ruisseaux sont embellis des fleurs écarlates de* Schizostylis coccinea (à gauche)*. Le Drakensberg est renommé pour ses immortelles;* Helichrysum adenocarpum (à gauche) *pousse haut dans les montagnes où ses feuilles et ses tiges velues la protège du froid extrême.*

The autumn-flowering bulbous plant, Empodium veratrifolium, *grows in rock crevices along the west coast of the Cape.*

Empodium veratrifolium *ist eine Knollenpflanze, die im Herbst blüht und in Felsenschluchten an der Westküste wächst.*

La plante bulbeuse Empodium veratrifolium, *qui fleurit en automne, pousse dans les fentes des roches le long de la Côte Occidentale.*

Struik Publishers (a division of New Holland Publishing (South Africa) (Pty) Ltd)
Cornelis Struik House, 80 McKenzie Street, Cape Town 8001

New Holland Publishing is a member of the Johnnic Publishing Group.
Visit us at **www.struik.co.za**

Log on to our photographic website ***www.imagesofafrica.co.za*** *for an African experience.*

First published 1996
Second edition 2003

10 9 8 7 6 5 4 3 2 1

Text © Colin Paterson-Jones 1996
Map © Struik Publishers 1996
Photographs © individual photographers and their agencies, as listed opposite.
Published edition © Struik Publishers 1996

Managing editor: Pippa Parker
Editor: Maggie Mouton
German translation: Friedel Herrmann
German editor: Bettina Kaufmann
French translation: Joyce Trocki
French editors: Bettina Kaufmann and Maggie Mouton
Design Manager: Petal Palmer
Designer and typesetter: Darren McLean
Cover design: Darren McLean
Map: Lyndall Hamilton
Reproduction by Unifoto (Pty) Ltd
Printed and bound by Kyodo Printing Co (Singapore) Pte Ltd

All rights reserved. No part of this publication may be reproduced, stored in a retrieval system or transmitted in any form or by any means, electronic, mechanical, photocopying, recording or otherwise, without the prior written permission of the copyright owners.

ISBN 1 86872 883 8

Photographic credits: ***Gerald Cubitt:*** *pp. 29 (bottom left), 36, 42 (top left), 42 (top right), 44 (top), 46 (bottom left);* ***Ian Davidson:*** *pp. 42 (bottom right); 46 (top);* ***R de la Harpe/SIL:*** *p. 38 (top);* ***Gerhard Dreyer/SIL:*** *front cover (top inset), pp. 20/21, 22 (top, 3rd from top, bottom), 22/23, 26 (bottom), 31 (left), 33 (top);* ***Lex Hes:*** *pp. 22 (2nd from top), 34, 35 (top right);* ***Landmarks/ Matthews:*** *pp. 15 (top), 35 (bottom left), 37 (bottom left), 41 (bottom);* ***John Manning:*** *pp.40 (top left), 45 (top);* ***NBI library:*** *p 37 (top);* ***Colin Paterson-Jones:*** *title page, pp. 4, 5, 6, 7, 8, 9, 10 (bottom right & bottom left), 11, 12, 12/13, 14, 15 (bottom), 16, 17, 18, 19, 21 (top right & top left), 24, 25, 28 (top, bottom right), 32 (top), 33 (bottom), 35 (bottom right), 37 (bottom right), 38 (bottom left), 39, 42 (bottom left), 43, 44 (bottom), 47, 48;* ***Linda Pithers:*** *pp. 28 (bottom left), 29 (right), 30, 35 (top left);* ***Lorna Stanton:*** *p 41 (top);* ***A E van Wyk:*** *pp 32 (bottom), 45 (bottom left);* ***A E van Wyk & S Malan:*** *pp. 40 (top right, bottom), 45 (bottom right), 46 (bottom right);* ***Hein von Hörsten:*** *pp. 2/3;* ***Lanz von Hörsten/SIL:*** *front cover, front cover (bottom inset), pp 10 (top), 26/27;* ***Zelda Wahl:*** *pp. 26 (top), 31 (top right), 38 (bottom right);* ***Keith Young:*** *p. 31 (bottom right).*

Front cover, main photograph: Namaqualand;
Top inset: *Gazania* sp.; bottom inset: *Lapeirousia silenoides*;
Title page: *Gloriosa superba* (Flame lily).